Glad to

D1647798

Dear
Jack —
May Eve always
inspire you!
In faith,
Rev.
Hoover

Glad to Be Human

Meditations by
Kaaren Solveig Anderson

Skinner House Books
Boston

Published by Skinner House Books, an imprint of the Unitarian Universalist Association, 25 Beacon Street, Boston, MA 02108-2800.

Printed in Canada.

ISBN 1-55896-404-5

05 04 03 02 01 00
10 9 8 7 6 5 4 3 2 1

Cover design by Suzanne Morgan.
Text design by kalzub design.

Library of Congress Cataloging-in-Publication Data

Anderson, Kaaren, 1966–
    Glad to be human : meditations / by Kaaren Anderson.
      p. cm.
    ISBN 1-55896-404-5
    1. Meditations 2. Spiritual life—Unitarian Universalist
Association. I. Title.
    BV4832.2 .A59 2000
    242—dc21

                                                           00-021174

To Solvay for giving laughter
To Nils for asking questions
To Scott for being grace

Contents

Eve's Muse

Describe Adam, you say. Well, he's kind of a wuss. Don't get me wrong, though, Adam's a nice guy. He just adheres to rules a little too strictly. Take his conversation with God before I was created. God tells my husband not to eat fruit from a tree in the center of the garden. Adam, unquestioningly goes along with the deal, "Sure God, I won't ever, ever touch that tree's fruit, cross my heart, hope to die."

That's Adam, just hanging out and enjoying this "paradise" as he calls it. Well, let me tell you, paradise wasn't nirvana. It was beautiful: luscious lakes, meandering rivers, verdant trees, prolific flowers, stunning mountains, but . . . boring. The Garden of Eden lost its appeal pretty quickly. It was nice not to have to work. It was nice essentially to have God wait on you hand and foot. Food was abundant, scenery ever wonderful, seventy degree days, light showers in the afternoon, and then back to perfect.

But, have you ever longed for something because life felt like a matzah cracker—dry and thin? Have you ever wanted something because you knew it would add spontaneity, diversity, and just plain change to your life? I did. Life sat pathetically before me on a silver platter. I didn't have to work, struggle, worry, engage, or contemplate. Life was supposedly perfect, and I was bored. Personally, I think God was bored too. Why else set up something to tempt so blatantly?

God also knew me. He knew I couldn't be stopped. He saw me bored out of my mind in that garden. Adam and I used to sit idly around, waiting for something to happen, anything to happen. I fell to twiddling my thumbs. Adam used to ask, "Is that all you know how to do?"

I'd tell him, "No, I can go this way too" and change the direction of my thumb twiddling. It got to the point where death didn't seem like such a bad alternative to boredom. At least monotony would get a run for its money.

Enter the snake. Smooth voice, pleasant serpent smile. A reptile that made sense. The snake reminded me that it was God who told Adam not to eat the apple. I was getting all my information secondhand.

"Remember," the snake reminded me, "Adam would rather stay in this so-called paradise with the same day, day after day, than to risk, or challenge, or imagine, or venture anything."

It was then that I looked into those snake's eyes and I saw my life. In great big capital letters, the irises of that snake read, *boring*. I saw myself and myself saw me. It was then that I knew I had to taste that apple. So, I did. I took a bite of that tart crispness. And all felt different. My body changed. I felt the sores on my feet. I felt a surge of life in my belly, my mind expand, my vision clear. For the first time, I felt whole. The spirit of life and love had consumed me. I felt wholly alive. Full of the spirit of God. So, I went to find Adam. I tried to explain how I felt. He just looked at me in horror and amazement, yet he kept asking me what it felt like. All I could think to say was, "I'm truly human. Adam, I feel more *me* than ever before!" I cajoled, argued, and finally just gave up. I shoved the apple into his taut mouth. He reluctantly took a bite. It was later that he told God it was all my fault.

Now here is the part of the story that I must confess needs correcting. I didn't blame the snake for my transgressions. I fessed up and admitted I had eaten the apple. I said in a proud, unwavering voice to God, "I am glad to be human! I can spurtle with rage, shake with despair, and bubble in ecstasy. Everything is not perfect, but it is real, alive! I feel sorry for you, God. For you everything is perfect, always going your way. Do you ever get bored? Want to be alive like me?"

Then God got mad. He cursed us both. He said that I would scream out in pain during childbirth, that I would regret the day I was born. But I must say, I never expected anything different after watching the animals in the garden give birth. They too suffered pain, yet had such a magnificent way to appreciate the outcome. We listened to the end of his tirade, and Adam just plopped down right there, looking out at everything he felt he had lost.

I picked up the apple and went to the gate. I stood there for a while, leaning against that cold wrought iron, throwing the apple up and down. Up and down. Up and down. I stood enjoying the rhythm of that apple slap into my hand, followed by silence as the air embraced it for a brief moment. Then slap. Then rest. Then slap. I looked out over the vast expanse of that wilderness, thinking about a song I had heard, "You can make the world your apple, take a bite before it sours, you can make the world your charm or your chain." I knew it lay before me, my life, my opportunity, my humanness. And I said out loud, in a clear voice, "I'm so glad to be human!"

Odiferous Beginnings

The other day I sat on the beach in literary frustration. My hardcover book was a detailed, brilliant, biting commentary on contemporary society. A double latte, coffee house kind of book. I should have grabbed a paperback "lush trash"–one more suitable to frequent interruptions and water-seeped defacement. In short, without the latte, my mind wandered. I escaped into eavesdropping. For the first time in a long time, I was thankful for teenage lamenting prattle. The topic: going back to school. Romantic in their revelry, four lanky high school boys brooded over the end to their undisciplined days, their perfect tans, and their daily preoccupation and rapture over the sixteen-year-old Venus lifeguard.

I joined their revelry. Daydreaming commenced. School days of old wafted across my thoughts with visions of new school clothes: sweaters, jeans, and boots. The fall kind of clothes we always wore on the first day of school despite an eighty-degree August swelter. Teachers, likable and unlikable, flickered before my eyes. And then I was bemused by an odiferous cacophony of memory. The smell of school. It was right before me, like a visual image, only more pungent. We all recognize that scent. It banters with you when you walk into any educational institution. The co-mingling of gym shoes, industrial cleanser, dime-store perfume, and rotting lockers. The smell that reminds me what time of year it is. But as I was thinking about school smells and autumn approaching, my mind turned. So did my nose. Another equally familiar, equally discernible odor, pierced my Nordic snoz. The aroma of church.

It's that time of year again. Yours is calling you back. When you walk in those doors on Homecoming Sunday, it's the odor that calls you back. Ours is not a gym locker, dime-store ingredient, crisp clothes kind of reek. No, the church odor is more of a strong perfume that beckons us back to new beginnings, to friends known and unknown, to history prophesied and history awakening. A delicate combination of our treasured yet timeworn building, warm, overcooked coffee, with a base note of the peculiar yet oddly familiar linger of laughter, tears, and thanksgiving. Open your windows and breathe deeply. Heed the beguiling aroma and follow your nose back to church. Come celebrate, rejoice together. Come. Breathe in the perfume of your church, your community, your home.

Mosquito

Sleep's blanket of respite eludes me. Mosquito bites line the arch of my left foot. The bed sheet scrapes my skin with remnant beach sand. The shade beats unevenly against the window sill. I can't sleep. I'm agitated. It doesn't help that the king of irritation buzzes slowly, persistently around my head. I put the covers over my head in an attempt to escape. But then, I can't breathe. I throw them off and come up for air. The impatient whine of the mosquito returns, torturing me, bumping into my temple, and retreating as I swat in vain into the surrounding darkness.

When I was a kid and still believed in God, I used to think mosquitoes were God's agitators. His way of making self-reflection a necessity, a chore.

I was always glad this agitation came in the darkness of the night, so no one else was privy to my tortured confessions. Mosquitoes could get me so uncomfortably awake that I became my own agitator. Agitating thoughts would swell in my head, rushing and reeling around me. Times in my life I wasn't so proud of me. Times I'd rather forget instead of remember. Times when I took advantage of a friend or misled a neighbor. Times I outright lied to cover my own failings, or spoke harshly when words of love were needed. I hated mosquitoes, they made me become my own tormentor. My own filter of conscience and good will. I wanted nothing more than to smash the little bugger buzzing around my head, as well as what was conjured up in my head.

I don't think mosquitoes are God's agitators anymore. I like to think of them as evolutionary justice. Imagine if you will, a mosquito during the dinosaur age. Bumping into those mammoth creatures, trying desperately to agitate, to irritate, to conjure self-reflection. Yet they were met with thick, impervious skin and brains so puny that consciousness-raising was never an option. Now, mosquitoes are in their element. They've come into their own. They feast on soft, gullible, permeable human skin. Skin that not only is sensitive, but captive to a body that holds a conscience, that can appreciate the agitation of the mosquito. A conscience that needs small irritating reminders that we can do better, reach for more, envision ourselves grander, kinder, more . . . well, likable.

Sleep is starting to sweep over me. The mosquito has had its fill. I close my eyes, and for the first time ever . . . have dinosaur envy.

A Good Unitarian

One summer evening, my kids and I ventured out to the cemetery for an after-dinner ramble. After walking about fifty yards on the cinder road, my son pulled me to the grass and asked me to read markers out loud to him.

"Mom, what does this one say?"

"Ah, Eugene Davidson, 1897–1963"

At every tombstone, he would stop, run his hand along the smooth, polished granite, and ask, "What does this one say?" I'd read the epitaph. We would talk about whether those resting below us had been young or old, male or female. He liked to speculate about the cause of their death.

Twenty-five markers later, my son tired of the process. He ran up behind his sister, tapped her on the head, and yelled, "Tag, you're it!" They wove quickly between markers, their heads bopping periodically into view. Then he stopped. Pointing at a marker, he called to me, "Mom, come look at this one. What does the one with the big 'T' on the top say?"

I caught up with him and smiled. "Emily Johnson, 1945–1973"

"Oh," he said, and tore off after his sister.

The big "T" on the top. For a split second, I imagined the cemetery with giant letters perched precariously on tombstone crests, weighing the consequences of falling to their fate, only to become graveyard alphabet soup. The image vanished. The big "T" was a cross. My next thought was, "Wow, my kid is a good Unitarian." He doesn't know the world through Christian eyes or symbols. He knows the world through Unitarian Universalist eyes. His symbol of religious identity is a flaming chalice. But it's not just the symbol that distinguishes my son, it's his use of the possible.

So often, my son's question about the big "T" would be proof positive to any "outsider" that we Unitarian Universalists raise ignorant children. It saddens me how many of us even fall into this trap. As adult Unitarian Universalists, or those who were raised UU, or seekers who are now moving on to a less questioning faith, often comment: "Well, what did it leave me with?", "I need more answers," or "UUs don't believe anything." Those who seek only concrete answers for a question end up labeling the rest of us as ignorant. And ironically, we even do it to ourselves.

But having eyes that can look at a tombstone with a cross on it as a big "T" allows us to do something far greater than sport our ignorance. It gives us the power to stand back and see the world through a variety of eyes. It gives us the opportunity to step back and see Jesus in a myriad of ways: myth, rebel, hero, agitator, visionary, or a plain old regular Joe. It gives us the ability to step back and see the universe as chaotic, comforting, random, or ordered. It gives us the freedom to imagine God as a bearded man sitting on a throne, a figment of our imagination, a noun, a verb, a grandfather, a mother.

So, I disagree. Our view doesn't leave one with nothing. It leaves one with something far more powerful and provocative. The power to enlarge the possible.

Zaine's Fairy Wings

Four years ago, I moved to a small town from New York City. At first I went through stimulus withdrawal: no fresh bagels on the corner, no intellectual frenzy of conversation, no subways and taxis. Now I get clean air and expansive starry skies. I still miss many of the people I knew in New York. Their robust spirits often took hold of my own, like Zaine.

Zaine was the little girl who lived on the top floor of my tenement. The year she was three, Zaine wore a crinoline slip under everything all year long. Her favorite outfit was a ruffled jean skirt, the crinoline peeping from under its hem. Black tights with multi-colored polka dots and pink high top Converse sneakers completed her getup.

But Zaine's ultimate fashion signature was her fairy wings. She wore them on Halloween and from that day forward. In the middle of winter, dressed in crinoline attire and bundled to the hilt, her fairy wings fluttered from the back of her winter coat. For one year, the wings never left her.

In my old neighborhood, folks didn't notice bizarre attire, or at least they pretended not to. People would outdo themselves to create unique looks. In New York, the odd is the norm and normal is odd. Nevertheless, in this neighborhood of eccentric folks, we all noticed Zaine. How could you not spot fairy wings?

Zaine served as the avatar of enlightened imagination. Zaine taught me to appreciate the capacity children have to be what they believe they can be. Zaine was a fairy that year, all year, living in whimsy wherever she went, the winged ideal of a free-spirited, uninhibited child.

Summer's languid days are dwindling. Schedules and order now take over. The back-to-school hubbub has started. Need evidence? Come with me to Walmart and marvel at aisles of shiny laminate binders and twelve-pack sets of No. 2 pencils. There, I am reminded of Zaine and start my quest for my own fairy wings. So far, no luck. But, I'm undaunted. When I do find them, I'll start a brigade. Any adult is welcome. You just need a desire to ignite that sacred childhood spark. But be forewarned: if you get there before me, just remember, the pink ones with silver glitter are mine.

Gerda's Raspberry

In August, I trekked to Boston for a day of books—my annual trip to browse, review, and buy inspirational and theological texts. After two hours, I started off for the train station. I wasn't in my typical hurry, so I stopped at the Holocaust Memorial, something I had previously walked quickly past. Names of hundreds of thousands of survivors towered over me, neatly written on giant plexiglass monuments. At eye level, sayings and quotes by survivors are etched into the structures. I got stuck in front of one. For five minutes, my feet cemented themselves to the pavement below me. I watched the construction workers eat their sandwiches from sturdy metal lunch boxes, listening to them discuss the intricacies of Sunday's football game. A busload of kids walked around me, engrossed in the woes of seventh-grade life.

But the world stopped for a while as I, feet still stuck, read and re-read the quote. Tears trickled out. Are there words to describe that feeling of horror that only a guttural, animalistic voice can reveal? An exhaling of breath that fights hard to return? Any memorial can do that to you, a witness and testament to injustice, pain, oppression.

I jotted down the quote on a piece of paper and brought it home. This tiny piece of paper received its own folder. I'd open it up, read the quote, and re-file, only to pick it up a few days later. It was magnetic. The words were by Gerda Weisman Klien: "Ilse, a childhood friend of mine, once found a raspberry in the camp and carried it in her pocket all day to present to me that night on a leaf. Imagine a world in which your entire possession is one raspberry and you give it to a friend."

I tried to imagine. I tried to put myself in Gerda's place, in Ilse's place. I couldn't. I would sit on the back steps of my house, eyes closed, trying to imagine the misery, the wonder of a such a gift, the selflessness of the act. I couldn't get there. Until one day with a raspberry pint resting in my lap, I'd lift one up and think of gifts given. Selfless giving by others: my mother's words of comfort the day I came home from school humiliated that I had been the first to misspell a word in the spelling bee; my sister's half smile and strong hands clenching mine as she whispered comforting words to me past drones of machines, pumps, and tubes during my ICU internment hell; my lover's words to me that to him I am Grace, I am Home. With each thought, I ate a raspberry. Something previously unimaginable now took shape, my vessel of life was full, filled with gifts. I felt Gerda's words and life in a way I couldn't comprehend before, by getting to the gifts that were given to me, all residing within, like well-eaten raspberries.

Ms. Perfect

Round, brown, doe-like eyes rested near the edge of her glasses. Best described as stout, there was nothing unhurried about her. The skin under her arms swung in pendulum force when she moved due to years of weight fluctuation. My grandmother. Far from a slave to fashion, she nonetheless cared about her appearance, wearing a full-corseted girdle daily. She wasn't ugly or beautiful, yet she sported a quick, one-sided mischievous grin that always kept you guessing as to her womanly guises. She was a klutz of enormous proportions, the trait I inherited. A woman who looked like a grandmother at thirty. It may not have helped that she drove a 1964 Plymouth Valiant with pushbutton transmission, the kind of car that no matter what your age screamed geriatric mobile.

My grandmother was a misfit of sorts. When I was a child, she was my icon of paradox. On one hand she was the mother of comfort. Her house always smelled of overcooked vegetables and well-used wool. When feeling out of sorts, she would promptly offer you her favorite food: Cheese Whiz on toast. On the other hand, nobody could embarrass me as a kid, making me uncomfortable like she could. She would be deep in conversation with someone while concurrently and unabashedly scratching her large bosom, oblivious to the obvious misstep in propriety.

She was queen of malaprop, which at times proved humorous and at others embarrassing. Once she was telling some friends of the family about my cousin's recent abode in Missouri, where she was attending college. "Well, Liv has found such a nice condom to live in, it's beautiful." It took everything in all of us gathered in her living room to bite any part of our mouth in an effort to control our laughter. The image of a house-sized latex condom serving as a condo had us in fits.

This odd woman could weave beauty into lives like none other. An avid, veracious quilter, she was a binder of pieces and parts. She took beauty seriously, and expected the rest of us to do so too. She was the most patient, attentive counselor. When burdened with life's questions and perplexities, her living room was always open, her ear always attuned, her answers measured. She could also give you a biting retort if she believed you to be slothy, unethical, or lazy in behavior.

My grandmother died ten years ago now. I miss her oddness, her quirky character. The older I get, the more I realize she had a lot to teach me—not in family history, or in how to be a quilter, or how to make carnage of fresh vegetables. No, the older I get, the more I think she was perfect. She wasn't a model with flawless features. She wasn't a Nobel Laureate, distinguished, astute, or brilliant. She wasn't even the nicest, kindest, gentlest person I knew. She was perfect because she knew how to be her—Sylvia Anderson. She knew how to be human, not a façade of one. There was no pretense about her, you got what you saw. She fit into her skin, and her skin fit her.

My own skin doesn't always fit so well. I get hung up on vanity, or trying to be hip or cool, or allowing conventional etiquette to rule my behavior or actions. I get in my own way of being me. My skin would fit better if I just remembered more often that wonderful woman I once knew and thought of her greatest gifts of being: contradiction, fallibility, and humor. The makings of a perfect gal.

One's Hands

A couple of weeks ago I was perusing football journals and books. I came across a photograph of a lineman. He was watching the field intently, his body hunched against a heavy sleet, his hands free to the elements. I turned the page of the book and there was a close-up of his hands, bent and mangled, covered with scabs, bruises, and scrapes. I was fascinated by his hands. Hands he would inevitably have to soothe. Hands that held violence and pain but also gentleness.

I put the book down and gazed at my own hands and thought about them: what they touch and experience and create. I already have my grandmother's hands with index fingers twisting slightly inward. I have bulbous veins winding under the skin that speak to my life: typing, playing the piano, soothing hurts, applying bandages, caressing, and daily work.

I like to look at farmers' hands or fishermen's hands. Laboring hands. Hands that speak to the life of the person. I don't want smooth hands; I want mine to speak to my person, to my life's work, to a sum of my parts. A place I can look and see generations before and after me, of work started or incomplete.

I have a colleague who is often present with people when they die. Once I asked her what she did. Did she have some ritual for the passing of a life? She said she helps wash the body. She washes the face as a symbol of what that person has seen, the hands as a symbol of what that person has done, and the feet as a symbol of where that person has been.

I love that symbolism. Unlike the lineman who can look at his hands and see what he does, most of us can forget what it is we do, and who we are connected to. But it's all there, in our hands. Those we touch or greet in welcome and friendship, of creation made possible through writing or painting or playing, of conversations retold, of tears shed in cradled hands.

The Shakers have a saying, "Hands to work, and Hearts to God." They believe that your life's calling—your work—should be no less than an act of joy. An act of work is an act of worship.

I stare at my hands and whisper, Amen.

Mr. Patton's Message

The other day, I was talking with a ten-year-old about band. He plays the trumpet. He asked if I had ever played in a band. I told him that I had joined the school band in seventh grade. I was first chair drummer. My band teacher was Mr. Patton. He was a replica of Santa Claus, though completely bald. For concerts, he would shine his head up so, as he said, he would "add some sparkle to the performance."

I had one big revelation in band: the importance of paying attention. If you asked any seventh grader what instrument they played, they would not only tell you what instrument, but were sure to extol the virtues of their own instrument. In their eyes, their instrument was the most important.

My friend Martha played the clarinet. She went on and on about the importance of the clarinet, how it often carried the melody and besides, it was quite handsome. Jackie played the flute. In her eyes, the flute was most important because it gave the band a sense of sleek, sanguine style. Yasmin played the saxophone and it added jazz. My friends, who were trombonists and tuba players, added depth and some bass. I, of course, thought the percussionists were most important. There would be no rhythm without us. In short, we all had an inflated view of the importance of our instruments.

On one particular day, we were all playing to the fullest of our capacities. In seventh grade this just meant volume. The doors to the music room began to shake. The louder we played, the more agitated Mr. Patton became. His face started glowing from his shirt collar up to the crown of his shiny, bald head. He looked like one of those hard candies called fire balls. Finally he snapped. His baton spiraled through the air, heading toward the tubas. The back of the wand nicked the bass drummer's elbow and skidded sideways to bounce off the top of a trombone. A jumble of toots and misnotes followed. We trailed off our playing, bewildered. What could we have done that could have angered him so? Then we found out.

Mr. Patton stood up to the fullest of his five-foot, six-inch potential and took an exaggerated deep breath. He then bore his vision into all of our rather confounded faces. "Okay, look you guys, those instruments you are playing have a higher purpose. Sure they each have individual merit, but you are part of a greater whole. That means that you need to do a few things. First, you need to respect one another's instruments. Contrary to what your inflated heads are all telling you, not one of you in this ensemble is more important than the other. Do you got that?"

We did. We nodded in unison. He continued, "Second, if we are going to create harmony, we need to cooperate. Repeat after me—co-op-er-ate." We all chanted back.

"And third," with some exasperation, "the cooperation and working together have to do mostly with this, so listen carefully!" He took a deep breath, "I'm the director here folks, so start paying attention. I shouldn't have to throw the baton to get you to look up here. *Wake up!* Quit sleeping through life on me! Got it?"

He was tired. We nodded in tandem. He took another deep breath, we took a deep breath. We started the piece over again.

If I believed in an omnipotent God, he would be like Mr. Patton. I think he had the divine intervention stuff down pretty well. He knew how to give it to us. He knew how to throw in some action, hurling batons and feisty, accrued anger over not paying attention. If I were God, that's what I would be mad about—the not paying attention part. Not noticing the morning dew, or how to work better together, to truly cooperate, instead of divide. Not realizing that we often are makers of our own misery, or that taking an afternoon nap can wake you up enough to notice how beautiful the maple tree is this year. That's what I would be mad at. Trying to wake everyone up and not having a lot of luck. I know one thing though, I'd be throwing a lot of batons.

Rev. Burkum's Bible

It's the season of Yom Kippur. A time during the Jewish calendar year to say you're "sorry" to not only those you've wronged, but the divine. A time of forgiveness, with the prospect of starting anew. And it's now that I remember.

When I was ten years old, we visited friends of the family. The father of the house was a very large, formidable Lutheran minister. He gave me a little Bible to look at. It was tiny, smaller than my palm, yet it was the Bible in its entirety. I could look at it, but I couldn't have it. Well, I took it. Okay, I stole it. I put it in my pocket and stole it. Later, I'd take it out to admire it, and honor would grab me and shake me. As if it were on fire, I would thrust it back in my desk drawer. I was a thief, of the Bible no less. Finally, I forgot my crime and the object of my shame.

When I was about fifteen and had outgrown the desk, I went through the drawers and found the minuscule Bible. I should have returned it then. I didn't. In fact, I decided not to deal with my emotions about the thing and threw it away. Sacrilege, I know, but it lay in the wastebasket on top of Kleenex and pencil shavings, mocking me. I pushed it to the bottom. Ugh.

Recently, I saw this minister at my sister's wedding. We had a great conversation. In the last couple of years, much grief has passed through his life. He spoke eloquently of my call and how proud of me he was. I couldn't tell him that, truth be told, I was a part-time Bible thief.

I often wonder why I felt so powerless that I acted out by stealing a Bible. I never enjoyed the act or the thing, and in the long run I just felt more powerless. I couldn't even tell him what I had done. I compounded the crime of my childhood with my silence. We adults don't like to feel powerless, or out of control, or wrong.

But, truth be told, I'm wrong a lot. Again: I'm wrong a lot. It is at this time of year, at Yom Kippur, that I'm forced to stand firm and look truth in the eyes and admit to my errors. Yom Kippur helps me look at my deepest darkest yuck and say, well, I'm wrong again, and then to ask for forgiveness, divine and human. It's an agitating holiday, not one that brings comfort and joy, or the promise of rebirth. No, Yom Kippur, I think, offers something deeper: the chance to be honest with ourselves, to touch the tip of our pain, to confront our insecurities, wantonness, abrasiveness, and powerlessness. It's a chance to become truly powerful. To face truth and ask for forgiveness for our imperfect humanity. We tend to mess up a lot. When we can admit that, we move forward and become more fully ourselves.

It's the season of Yom Kippur. I have a wrongdoing list to attend to. Forgiveness to ask for. I just wish the first name didn't start with a Rev.

"Places, Places, Please!"

In December I journey to Chicago to perform the wedding of one of my best friends, an actress of striking good looks and commanding confidence. She has a strong presence, a dancer's long stride, and perfect posture. I stand with hips out and have a slouchy walk. I am four inches taller than she is, but I often feel shorter. We make a great pair.

At the rehearsal, I realize that I am the only one in the wedding party who is not a professional actor. And I don't mean actors as in I-wait-tables-and-call-myself-an-actor actors. These are working actors: six Broadway actors, one soap opera star, and a movie and sitcom actress. I am in the company of true thespians.

The hubbub starts. Groomsmen call out, "Places, places, please." Bridesmaids admonish, "Quiet on the set." The bride and groom stomp around, clapping their hands and exclaiming, "Let's go people, chop, chop!" I, the one who is supposed to be running the show, am being manipulated, manhandled, and upstaged! After the places and blocking, the run-through begins with what they call the overture, a medley of show tunes. People move to their marks, walk in practiced step down the stairs, and read their words with resonant tone and measured speech. I don't utter a word. I never get the chance. There is stiff competition for my role. In the end, I mumble, "This is supposed to be a spiritual event folks, not an audition." I am a director without direction.

Next day, wedding day, I arrive at the house and go upstairs to find my friend. The room is filled with women in their twenties and thirties in drop-dead outfits. This company of decked-to-the-hilt modelettes surely required the aid of butter knives to enter their dresses. My friend's wedding dress, a cream satin, complete with opera gloves, was designed by the costume designer on her recent tour. She looks stunning, as all brides do. Dressed for my role as minister in a demure blue suit, I am feeling frumpier by the minute.

I go downstairs and stroll casually through the assembling congregation. The hairdresser and his wares monopolize the dining room table. His shoulder-length hair is feathered and lacquered solid like a seventies country singer. His assistant's hands are a riot of rhinestones and gold, and chime as he swiftly hands combs and brushes. One large guest in her (his?) sixties is standing next to me in a long black sequin gown, an eight-foot black feather boa draped exotically over her shoulders, and three-inch eyelashes splashed with silver glitter. Then the women in their seventies arrive, all wearing skirts that leave nothing to the imagination. The grandmother of the groom is most memorable: miniskirt, bright red stockings, black stiletto heels, and a vampish cigarette holder. (If my legs happen to be that shapely when I'm seventy, forgive me if the navy suit hangs unused in my closet. The heads can turn to me, officiating minister.)

The wedding starts. Show tunes call everyone to their places. The mothers walk down the elegant staircase, gowns dancing in time to the music. Then my friend enters, looking radiant. Everyone is in place. There is quiet on the set. I start the ceremony.

The wedding is very emotional. My friend and her partner say their vows to one another with great vigor and intention. They both start sniffling. Then the soap opera star launches into Shakespearean monologue. Drama fills the air. My friend's soon-to-be husband shivers with emotion. Tears don't trickle lightly from his eyes; they cascade. He is in need of a rain gutter. The soap opera star joins in. It occurs to me that either they are exceptional actors or they are deeply moved. I opt for the latter. I myself start to lose my composure, my eyes pooling. The soap opera star stops mid-sentence to gather himself. The room is filled with sniveling, quiet snorts, and sharp, in-drawn breaths.

A video camera is pointed directly at me, capturing each precious moment on tape. My eyes are teary and red, my make-up smeared. By this time, the glamor is gone. And my nose is running. Dripping on my stole, I ask myself how I'm feeling, "Humbled? Humiliated? Raw?"

I am not alone. There is no pretense left. No superficiality. There is a new camaraderie between stranger and friend, as tissues are passed from one hand to another. Surprised by our own humility, by our own vulnerable selves, exposed so severely to one another, we are privileged to witness a simple act—love shared and given. And at that moment, it doesn't matter that these are professionals, that everyone makes their cues, or that the costumes are beautiful. What matters is two naked souls, expressing the love that makes the world move. I stand aside following the service and let myself feel the full spin of the earth, moving quicker in that moment, and smile.

Ding-a-ling-a-ling!

When I was a child, the day after Thanksgiving was steeped in ritual. Every year my family would travel to Chicago for the holiday festivities. Our tour was always the same: We'd tromp up and down Michigan Ave., admiring store windows with animated mechanical dolls that served as actors for the narrated holiday story. We would wait in line for two hours to sit under the three-story tree at Marshall Fields and enjoy a formal lunch, and sit on Santa's lap to discuss the finer points of our list. Then on to the Berghoff for dinner.

The day always held magic, mostly because of my dime-laden mittens. In the morning, my dad would give my sister and me each a handful of dimes, which I kept in my mittens so I could tinker with them as we walked in anticipation of finding another one of "them"—Salvation Army Christmas buckets. At almost every corner familiar red cans awaited. I marveled in watching my dimes swirl their way to the quarter-sized slot and plunk in to rest amid other dime-sized donations. At the time, I knew nothing about Salvation Army theology, only that they worked for the homeless and destitute. They became my symbol of generosity for the season, albeit bucket-sized.

As an adult, I often felt an odd pull to ring the bell myself. One year I gave in. I called up the lieutenant at the local Salvation Army and asked enthusiastically if they were in need of help. They were. I was given two assignments. I couldn't wait to get my hands on that little tinkly bell.

The first assignment was a busy street corner with a bookstore and coffee shop on either side. I rang my ding-a-lingy bell in ten-degree weather with glee, stamping my feet periodically to stay warm. My smart bucket swung slightly in the breeze. It was an experience just as I had hoped: people asked me if I was warm enough, a couple bought me coffee, many smiled and simply wished me "Happy Holidays" as they passed. I marveled at the parade of dime donors and the familiar "plunk" of change that followed.

The second assignment was at a mall across from JC Penney's. Once again eager, I itched to start my ring-a-dinging. The lieutenant arrived to set up my bucket. My hands reached for the bell. No bell. He explained, "The mall owners have complained, no bells, only this." He handed me a sign.

The sign was attached to a long dowel. On the top of the dowel, two pieces of paper were stapled together over the center of the stick. One side read "DING," the other "DONG." Instead of ringing, I now had to flip a sign that read "DING-DONG." My little bucket instantly lost its ting-a-ling. My enthusiasm waned. I flipped in silent motion. It seemed absurd, but I went to work. People pushed past each other, mired in that Christmas hubbub that leans toward frustration, not joy. Then they'd spot me. Their faces would contort, scrunching up into laughter and that uncomfortable feeling when you're embarrassed and humored by someone at the same time. They would often throw in some dimes and say "Happy Holidays," barely able to stifle an awkward yet justifiable smirk. I fought hard not to feel like the sign was projecting my mental state to the mall community.

For four hours I flipped—the sign, that is. Ten minutes before I was to quit, this fellow in black cowboy boots and a ten-gallon hat walked up to me and laughed. He was full out chuckles, bent over, hysterically laughing. I stood taller, flipping my sign with increased vigor. I couldn't tell where he was going with this. When he finally stood up for air, his eyes were smiling, so I hoped for no malicious intent. But I also was ready to kick him in the shins for his reaction to me and my now stupid sign.

Then he said, "I must say, I've never seen a sign like that before. Anybody that stands with a sign that says 'Ding-Dong' must be duly rewarded." He reached into his back pocket and retrieved his wallet. Crisp bills lay neatly in uniform order. He ran through the fives, tens, and twenties, and got to a row of fifties. He pulled one out. A fifty. He neatly folded the bill and squeezed it into the bucket designed for coin donors. Nodding, he smiled right into my eyes and muttered, "Well, I never." Then he continued on through the mall with laughter that hung captive in the air like lingering pipe smoke.

I, on the other hand, began to turn that sign with a renewed vigor. I looked at each passerby with a new attitude, whether they snickered or smiled, donated or not. I now felt strangely in awe of my DING-DONG sign. I was unabashedly proud that I was stupid enough to stand in a mall tenaciously flipping a sign, waiting for humor and generosity to awaken someone's humdrum spirit. Waiting for it to finally dawn on me that my gifts of generosity and time needed to lose their pretenses in order for any true generosity to occur. Waiting, just to discover, that this season can still thrill and surprise. Waiting for magic, only to find that red buckets held it all the time. Even without the ding-a-ling.

Head Butting

A couple of weeks ago Santa was checking his list, finding out who was naughty or nice. Carefully analyzing Midwestern entries, he came upon a list from a fellow in Wisconsin named Brian, a nice enough fellow in his twenties, whose list contained two words. Santa read the words, gave a slight shiver, and decided he couldn't fill the order appropriately. He quickly wrote a note to Brian's girlfriend. He feigned an allergic reaction to the gift in question, professed a fear for the object of desire, and apologized for not being able to fill the order. Then he neatly folded the letter, stuffed it in a little red envelope, and addressed it to my sister Ingrid.

While singing a little Christmas ditty to herself, she received the letter from Santa. She stopped singing upon looking at Brian's two-word request. After a slight shiver, she decided that if Santa couldn't accommodate, then she would. She would buy her boyfriend, her roommate, the present—a ball python.

Just a nice little snake that measures about five feet in length, about four to five inches in girth, and eats small yet live mice for dinner. Just the kind of fun-loving pet you too would want in your one-bedroom apartment. Yet some mystical spirit invaded her body and she bought him the snake.

Feeling comfortable in my humble, yet snake-free abode, I thought why in God's name would someone want a five-foot snake around their house. I could imagine it, coiling around my sister's leg in her sleep, constricting her, making sleep and sweet dreams improbable. I shuddered, now understanding Santa's reluctance to fulfill Brian's request.

So I called up Brian and asked—Why? After he spent ten minutes extolling my sister's virtues for buying him the dreadful creature, I prodded him, "Brian, I don't get it, it's a snake for God's sake."

"Beautiful creatures," he remarked. "This particular snake has a base color of dark brown, and is patched with a tan all along its topside. Spots really, but bigger, creating a beautiful pattern." He continued, "Ball pythons have a mellow temperament and are considered docile. They get their name because when they are frightened or sleeping, they coil up into a three-dimensional ball, hence the name Ball Python."

I was intrigued most by how these snakes shed their skin. They start by butting their face against something to get the peeling process going. Then they rub against something rough, or along the side of their quarters, helping the skin to roll off in one piece. They do this process monthly, not annually.

I like the image of head butting to start a peeling process, especially at Christmas time. Seems ironic really.

How often we butt our heads against a wall over traditions that we detest, frustration with obligatory gift giving when we would rather not, or trying to find joy in the midst of feeling overwhelmed. Uff. Seems this time of year needs a good case of head butting. Head butting that leads to peeling away resentful obligation, desires for ongoing magical moments, and the fear that Martha Stewart will always one-up us every year. So what, I say. If you start head butting in early December, the peeling process will begin. A shedding of fear and control and anxiety over all being perfect. I think head butting's a necessity, a must, or we end up just left in our layers of dead skin. Our out-of-date traditions and habits and behaviors. So hey, it's head-butting season. Let the peeling begin.

Reluctant Goodbyes

I hate goodbyes. I hate everything about them. It bothers me that "goodbye" isn't really what I think we most often want to say.

When those I love leave me, or I leave them, goodbye isn't what I want to say. I want to tell them that their warm hand on my cheek, which caught my desperate tears, made me feel whole once again. I want to tell them that without their quick giggle and tender words, my life can feel lonely. But no—instead I tell them, "I love you," give them a hug, and say goodbye. And they leave and I leave. I feel hollow, discontented, and sometimes lost. I didn't want to say goodbye.

When those I am in conflict with leave or I leave them, goodbye isn't what I want to say. I want to talk about pieces of me that are torn, scratched, and fragmented because of our interchanges. I want to tell them that, just maybe, I've learned something new: in how to be, in how to live, in how to grow. I wonder why it got so complicated and sticky. But no—instead we say with fortitude, "Goodbye." I may shake their hand, glad that I won't have to see them again. But there is so much unsaid, and goodbye doesn't skim the root of my feelings. I didn't want to say goodbye.

When time whispers to me, "Move on, here's the next step, say goodbye," I watch as my son walks into his first day of kindergarten, confident, filled with anticipation. These are my people, my life, he is thinking.

"Bye, mom," he yells to me and signs *love*. I sign back.

"Bye," I whisper. But goodbye isn't what I want to say. I want to tell him that he is remarkable, brave, that I need more time to adjust to his boyhood, his self-assurance, his friends. I need more time to let go of one more tiny sliver of him. But no—instead I say goodbye. I feel jolted, awakened to time moving forward without me. I didn't want to say goodbye.

When someone I love dies, goodbye isn't what I want to say. I want to tell them the truth about us. I want to set it straight. Get to what was real. That their words could hurt, that I wasn't as strong as they'd hoped, that I still struggle to forgive them. At the same time, I want to tell them that their love made life easier, freer, more accessible. That I'm grateful for their presence. I want to tell them that I forgive them for being human, hoping they did the same for me. But no—instead we say "goodbye" at a memorial service. And I feel captured in a storm of emotions that violently swirl me around. I didn't want to say goodbye.

When life turns to me someday and says, "Say goodbye," goodbye isn't what I want to say. I'll say, "I've said 'Goodbye' my whole life, let me say it right, now. Just let me say it right." But life's hands will close around me, ushering me to something new. It will be the only time where "goodbye" was what I needed to say.

The Kindness of Lo Mein

My friend Marcy and her boyfriend Brian recently ate dinner at a local Chinese restaurant. As they enjoyed a plate of lo mein, engrossed in conversation, a hand reached down and ushered away their platter of noodles. A voice quick and agitated mumbled "Sorry!" and a thin, poorly dressed woman left the restaurant with their plate of lo mein.

In astonishment, they watched her walk down the street, holding the plate with the flat of her hand as she stuffed noodles into her mouth, slapping sharply against her face. The owner realized what had happened and darted out the front door, chasing after the noodle thief. He stood firmly in front of her, blocking her way and grabbing a side of the plate. A struggle ensued, noodles slid uneasily from one side to the other, slopping over the edge. He surged forward and pulled with a heroic strong-arm attempt to retrieve his plate. The woman's fingers slid from the plate. Noodles flew, then flopped pathetically on the sidewalk.

Left empty-handed, with soggy, contaminated noodles at her feet, the woman stood with arms hung dejectedly at her side. The owner walked victoriously back to the restaurant with the soiled plate in hand. My friends were given a new heaping plate of lo mein, although they had already consumed half of the stolen plate. A stream of apology in Chinese came from the proprietor. Unable to eat anymore, they asked to have the noodles wrapped up and set off to see their movie.

A block later, they happened upon the lo mein thief. The woman was hypercharged. She simultaneously cried, convulsed, and shouted at a man, who rapidly retreated from her side. My friend, unsure about what to do, listened to her boyfriend's plea to just walk away. But she didn't. Instead, she walked over to the thief and said, "Ah, we haven't formally met, but about ten minutes ago, you were interested in our noodles. They gave us some new ones, are you still hungry?" The woman nodded and extended her bony arms. She took the styrofoam container in her hands, bowed ever so slightly, and murmured, "Thank you, you're very kind."

What makes us walk away from discomfort? Or stay? You could say a lot about my friend's story—a lot about generosity, kindness, attention, and thievery. I'm more interested in what motivates us to confront that which makes us uncomfortable and makes us look at the guts and grit of decisions, the choices to not address things that are uncomfortable, uneasy, unbalanced, unnatural, unbelievable. When our foundations start to shake, we can feel the tremors move up our legs and into our torsos. And we want more than anything to make it stop. Any how. Any way.

My friend Marcy could feel herself shake. I know because she told me so. But she chose not to walk away, she dealt with uncomfortableness. She held firm in the muck. Sometimes, that's all we need or can do to get to the other side—the side where generosity, comfort, and kindness reside, the side where foundations are firm and stable. Where one's shaking walks back to the other side.

Piecing the Quilt

My friend Marcy is a tough woman: a lawyer by trade, opinionated, erudite. She is not one you mess with. On occasion she can exhibit a tender side. She can sing you to sleep with a seventies pop medley that stretches her range (vocally) and your own as to what is comforting. She has an uncanny ability to laugh at herself and life. But, sappy? Never. Not her. At least, I didn't think so until I heard the story of her childhood quilt.

Marcy is one in a family of five kids. As a kid, she relied on a yellow and white quilt for security. Given to her at her birth, she carried it around with her wherever she went: grocery shopping, to the movies, to Grandma's . . . she was a regular Linus. One day her mother decided that she was sick of seeing this undoubtedly worn, dirty, scraggly blanket. If my experience at all matches hers, Marcy's mother was mostly sick of looking for it, in those hours of panic and loss, as she ran around the house searching under couches, chairs, in closets, cupboards, hoping to end her daughter's whining. She was determined to wean her daughter of the blanket.

Once a week, for about six months, Marcy's mother would snip off parts of her blanket, making it smaller and smaller. Marcy said if nothing else it got easier to carry, and was serving its purpose, at least from her mother's perspective. At the end of six months, Marcy was left with a palm-size blanket. She continued to use it through her nightly medley to her sisters. She'd still pull the fabric through her forefinger and thumb, in a slow rhythmic fashion. She persisted in sleeping with the remnant of her quilt, a small vestige of comfort and childhood days gone by.

When she told me this story, I was in tears—the image of this child with a now two-inch-by-two-inch blanket had me in fits of laughter. I could just picture her rubbing the piece of fabric against her cheek and inhaling the comforting aroma. I don't think I need to remind you that most children's blankets get odiferous pretty quickly considering they manage to wipe, rub, and spill everything on them. But Marcy says, "I loved that smell." In truth, I was amazed that the cutting of the blanket didn't bother her that much. As long as she had a piece of her quilt left, she was quite content.

Most of us are like my friend Marcy with a two-inch-by-two-inch quilt that says this is who I am. A piece that needs the community spirit of ministering to one another, to make it into a whole piece, a quilt. Some of our pieces are in need of repair, of healing, of patching. They need to be sewn or mended. Others show signs of care already taken with minute, careful, precise stitches. Still others are fixed with Scotch tape or staples. I like to think of church as a gathering place to bring our shredded and worn quilt pieces together—to share. It is in this symbolic action of piecing our lives and stories together into one, in all our diversity of pieces, that makes our quilts whole and healing. Not only for ourselves, but for all of us who will get the benefit of the quilt when we are most broken, most in need of care.

When we come together to piece and sew and mend, we bind ourselves to one another, taking that which makes us most human to share with our pew mates. That is the work of the real quilter, putting the pieces together. Every now and then I get glimpses of the quilt of my church. It is most satisfying when everyone has taken out their needles to explain, revise, and exemplify various mending techniques or sewing skills. Piecing one life to another. Binders, quilters, we.

The Cat Lady

May Day was a religious institution in my family. My father imparted the tradition of May baskets at a young age, and we never missed the event until I was a sophomore in high school. Each April 30 or so, we would trek down to Guth's Candy on Main Street and carefully select barrel candy for our neighbor's basket. Racing home with our soon-to-be-distributed stash, we discussed hiding spots, and whose house would get the sacred honor of being first. On the first of May, construction paper baskets lined the wagon, overflowing with hard candy, popcorn, and Wisconsin Wood Violets.

Tradition held that baskets were left on someone's front doorknob. You then rang their doorbell and ran away quickly to hide in the bushes at the edge of the lot to wait. Most neighbors followed a predictable pattern. Agitated, they'd stomp out to the porch and look around for the vile youth engaging them in what they thought was an unfriendly game of ding-dong ditch. But eventually they'd spot the benign basket hanging on their doorknob. Smiling now, their eyes scanned the yard for suspects as they gently picked the basket from the handle and retreated inside, as if embarrassed that they had thought the worst.

Conversely, if you knew the tradition, like my neighbor, you wore your running shoes in anticipation. Tradition held that when a May basket was left, the occupant of the house had to run after the child in question and shower them with affection in thanks for their generosity. In my neighbor's case, that meant getting kissed all over your face like an enthusiastic adolescent Lab. You were left with a dewy residue as an emblematic symbol of his thankfulness and virility.

I never outran my neighbor David until I was a freshman in high school. By that time he was in his late fifties, and as I saw it, youth had its advantages (I got tackled hard by his twenty-something son that year—I hadn't managed to outrun the whole family yet).

My sister and I kept one person on our list for last—an elderly woman who wore mismatched clothes and house slippers. At least I thought they were house slippers, but it was hard to tell because she rarely left her house long enough to breathe in fresh air. When she did, she parked her big, foreboding red Cadillac at the bottom of her side stairs only to slide into her house, leaving the neighborhood kids thirty-second glances at best. She lived with her equally reclusive husband, and together they shared a house with twenty or so cats.

Every year my emotions were mixed about going to her house, the dominate emotion being discomfort. My dad, however, gently coaxed us on, encouraging us to not forget the "cat lady." He never insisted, just expressed his opinion that "it might be a good idea, that's all."

And every year, my fear vanished with her reaction. With doorbell rung, she'd walk out her front door, holding the door wide for two or three cats to ramble out for joint inspection. Her hands would fly up in jubilant surprise. Swiping the basket, she too would scan the yard, but then yell out *"Thankkkkkk youuuu!"*—loud enough for the entire neighborhood to hear. Hoisting up one of her cats, she then discussed the contents of the basket with the cat, as if it understood perfectly, leaving us privilege to each little, "ooooh" and "aaaah" and "Oh my, isn't this just exquisite!" She would tuck the wood violets behind her ear, only to disappear into her house once again to become the mysterious "cat lady."

I never once walked home without feeling grand somehow. All our efforts were met in that single *"Thankkkkkk youuuu!!"* The "cat lady" was an odd duck in some ways. Up until her, our route included generosity to those who were comfortable, neat, and orderly. Her thank you was an added benefit. But the grand piece of life came from our own need to verify that generosity need not play to a perfect house. Her thank you was a nice added touch, but in truth, it's what the act did to me that made life grand. Her house made the whole event meaningful. Her house changed our sweet little generous act to something larger. All because it wasn't so neatly put together. She changed me, expanded me, challenged me. I think of her now and can only think to yell back, *"Thankkkkkk youuuu!"*

Walking the Wire

At a conference recently, our small group was asked to define a word, then give it a motion. Our word: courage. Our definition: the ability to take risks. Our motion: a tightrope walker, about to step out onto the rope.

The tightrope image. It often passes through my mind at the most peculiar place—the graveyard. The other day, I walked through Old First Parish Burying Grounds, across from the beach. I read epitaphs. The sky was uncharacteristically blue, the wind mellow. I stood on the hill overlooking the beach, the ground firm, sturdy below my feet. I went to the cemetery in search of risk takers, livers of lives, wholeness finders. The remains of the folks beneath my feet had lived as I, for they had breathed, and ate, and slept. But, I wanted to know, had they risked? Their epitaphs didn't help.

One marker spoke of the fellow's virtues. But most, especially the women's, read plainly. "Martha Smith, wife of Jonathan Smith, born 1789–died 1854." I thought it too bad we don't put more detail on our grave-stones. I wanted to know how the fellow was virtuous. Had he ever risked anything? Had he risked disappointing another to be true to himself? Had he bared the accusation of a betrayal to not betray his own soul? Had he ever risked failure and was still able to yell a resounding "Yes!" to the universe?

Now, I'm not suggesting nor embracing shaking up lives with mindless or needless risk taking. Writer Norman Cousins said, "In short, freedom's main problem is the problem of the individual who takes himself lightly historically." He's right. Most of us, if not everyone I know, will not make it into the history books. Our lives will not be emulated or reviewed or critiqued by a fifth-grade history class. But I don't think we give ourselves enough credit. History is just the retelling of a particular event in time. When we die, we remain alive in the hearts and memories of one another's very beings. We are reflected in one another because we can be the spirit that animates life when we risk loving, caring, and especially failing.

I'm not especially brave or courageous. Chances are slim that I'll walk on a tightrope, bungee jump, become president, or engage in international espionage. Risky jobs or avocations. But that's not what I'm talking about. Not adventure as much as your ability to probe the truth, to live with integrity, to encompass compassion, to be bold in living and loving. Risky, courageous endeavors.

When people amble through a graveyard in a hundred years, I want them to stop at my tombstone, befuddled over a simple sketch: a drawing of a tightrope walker taking the first step. They may think that's what I did with my life. But no. How they would be surprised to know that all I did was to risk love and boundaries, truth and failure. That's all I will have done. But that will not go on my tombstone if I fail to earn the right to have it there. So I remind myself of that tightrope each day. You have the same one before you. Take a step. Be bold. And don't forget to breathe.

Unitarian Universalist Meditation Manuals

This list includes all meditation manuals since the merger in 1961. For information about meditations prior to 1961, contact Skinner House Books, 25 Beacon Street, Boston, MA 02108.

2000   *Glad to Be Human* Kaaren Anderson
        Out of the Ordinary Gordon B. McKeeman

1999   *The Rock of Ages at the Taj Mahal*
          Meg Barnhouse
        Morning Watch Barbara Pescan

1998   *Glory, Hallelujah! Now Please Pick Up Your Socks*
          Jane Ellen Mauldin
        Evening Tide Elizabeth Tarbox

1997   *A Temporary State of Grace* David S. Blanchard
        Green Mountain Spring and Other Leaps of Faith
          Gary A. Kowalski

1996   *Taking Pictures of God* Bruce T. Marshall
        Blessing the Bread Lynn Ungar

1995   *In the Holy Quiet of This Hour*
          Richard S. Gilbert

1994   *In the Simple Morning Light* Barbara Rohde